975.1
MIL

Miller, Amy.

Delaware.

$29.50   3254716011862

DATE			

FROM SEA to SHINING SEA

DELAWARE

AMY MILLER

Consultants

MELISSA N. MATUSEVICH, PH.D.
Curriculum and Instruction Specialist
Blacksburg, Virginia

ELIZABETH SIMMONS
Youth Services Librarian
New Castle County Library System
Wilmington, Delaware

JENNIFER L. MINCHINI
Children's Librarian
Brandywine Springs Elementary School
Wilmington, Delaware

CHILDREN'S PRESS ®
A DIVISION OF SCHOLASTIC INC.

New York • Toronto • London • Auckland • Sydney • Mexico City
New Delhi • Hong Kong • Danbury, Connecticut

Delaware is in the northeastern part of the United States. It is bordered by Pennsylvania, Maryland, New Jersey, and the Atlantic Ocean.

The front cover photo shows the Hagley Museum on Brandywine Creek.

Project Editor: Meredith DeSousa
Art Director: Marie O'Neill
Photo Researcher: Marybeth Kavanagh
Design: Robin West, Ox and Company, Inc.
Page 6 map and recipe art: Susan Hunt Yule
All other maps: XNR Productions, Inc.

Library of Congress Cataloging-in-Publication Data

Miller, Amy.
   Delaware / Amy Miller.
     p. cm. — (From sea to shining sea)
   Includes bibliographical references and index.
   ISBN 0-516-22482-4
   1. Delaware—Juvenile literature. [1. Delaware.] I. Title. II. Series.
F164.3 .M55 2002
975.1—dc21   2001006982

TABLE of CONTENTS

CHAPTER ONE

INTRODUCING THE FIRST STATE

Flags outside the capitol building commemorate December 7, 1787, the day Delaware approved the United States Constitution.

Delaware is a small state, but it has played a big part in American history. Swedish and Dutch settlers were the first Europeans to arrive in the land we now call Delaware, and it became one of England's thirteen colonies. After the American Revolution, Delaware was the first state to approve the United States Constitution. That's why Delaware is also known as the First State.

There's more to Delaware than history. Today, some of America's largest banks and corporations have their headquarters in Delaware. Farming is also big business in the state. Delaware farmers grow vegetables such as peas and soybeans, and raise broiler chickens. In fact, the first broiler chickens in the United States were raised in Delaware.

What comes to mind when you think of Delaware?

❖ Native Americans hunting, fishing, and farming
❖ Henry Hudson exploring the mighty Delaware River

- Swedish and Dutch settlers building the first log cabins in the Americas
- Fierce pirates terrorizing small seaside towns in the 1700s
- Caesar Rodney riding 80 miles (129 kilometers) on horseback to cast his vote for American independence from England
- Herons and geese feasting on fish and shellfish in national wildlife refuges
- Companies conducting business around the world from their headquarters in Wilmington
- Sun-lovers playing and relaxing on beautiful beaches
- Race cars tearing up the track at Dover Downs International Speedway

There's something for everyone in Delaware, whether you love history, the outdoors, or race cars. In this book, you'll learn about some of the people and events that have helped to develop the First State. Turn the page to discover the story of Delaware.

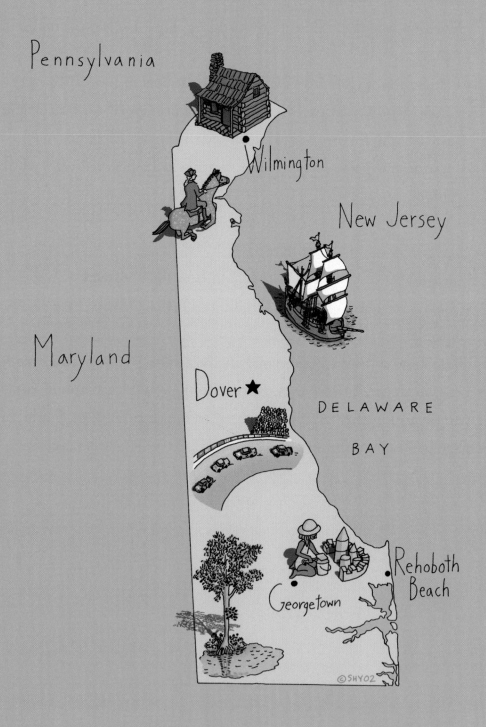

Pennsylvania

Wilmington

New Jersey

Maryland

Dover ★

DELAWARE

BAY

Rehoboth
Beach

Georgetown

©SHY02

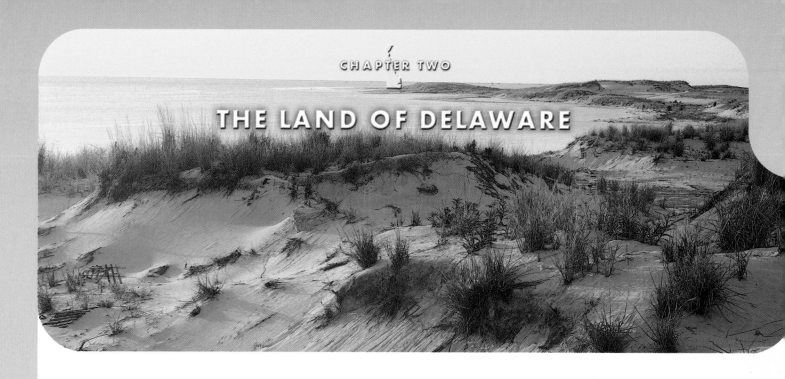

CHAPTER TWO

THE LAND OF DELAWARE

Where is Delaware? If you look on a map, you'll see that it is located in the northeastern part of the United States, on the eastern half of the Delmarva Peninsula. A peninsula is a piece of land that is surrounded by water on three sides. Maryland and Virginia also occupy part of the Delmarva Peninsula, which is surrounded by the Chesapeake and Delaware Bays. The peninsula is named for these three states: *Del*aware, *Mar*yland, and *Virgin*ia.

To the east of Delaware is the Delaware River, Delaware Bay, and the Atlantic Ocean. New Jersey is across the Delaware River. To the north lies Pennsylvania and to the west is Maryland. Delaware's border with Maryland runs through two towns: Delmar and Marydel. Delaware also has several small islands located along the shore, such as Pea Patch, Reedy, and Fenwick Islands.

The sandy beaches and marshes of Cape Henlopen State Park are one of Delaware's many popular recreational spots.

EXTRA! EXTRA!

Delaware's border with Pennsylvania is the only border between two states formed by the arc, or curve, of a perfect circle. It is called the Twelve-Mile Circle because every point along the border is 12 miles (19 km) from the Old Court House in New Castle.

If you're not careful, you might overlook Delaware on a map. Delaware covers only 2,489 square miles (6,446 square kilometers). It is the second smallest state in the United States—only Rhode Island is smaller. In a car, you could travel the entire length of Delaware in less than two hours. It is only 96 miles (154 km) from north to south. You could drive across the state in less than one hour. Its greatest distance from east to west is 35 miles (56 km). In some places, Delaware is only 8 miles (13 km) wide!

GEOGRAPHIC REGIONS

Delaware is made up of two geographic regions: the Atlantic Coastal Plain and the Piedmont Plateau. Most of Delaware lies within the Atlantic Coastal Plain, an area that stretches along the East Coast of the United States from New York to Florida. It is mostly flat land with only a few low hills. Delaware has the lowest elevation in the United States—60 feet (18 m) above sea level.

Delaware has many wet, muddy areas called saltwater

FIND OUT MORE

There are three types of plains: coastal plains, inland plains, and flood plains. Coastal plains slope gently toward the sea. Inland plains are found away from the coast, usually in the middle of a land mass. Flood plains are formed from mud and sand left by the overflow of a river. Where can you find each of these plains in the United States?

marshes. Some of these marshes reach several miles inland in Delaware. When these marshes are overgrown with trees and shrubs they are called swamps. What remains of the Great Cypress Swamp can be found in southern Delaware. At one time, this swamp covered more than 50,000 acres (20,234 hectares) of land.

Not all of Delaware is made up of marshes and swamps. Miles of sunny beaches line Delaware's southern coast. Millions of sun-loving

Saltwater marshes cover much of Bombay Hook National Wildlife Refuge in Smyrna.

One of the best ways to explore the coast of Delaware is by taking a bike ride along the Coastal Heritage Greenway.

tourists enjoy these beaches each year. It is also a great place for fishing. Commercial fishermen and chartered boats catch saltwater fish in Delaware Bay and the Atlantic Ocean.

At the northeastern tip of Delaware, rolling hills rise from the flat Atlantic Coastal Plain. These hills are part of a wide plateau called the

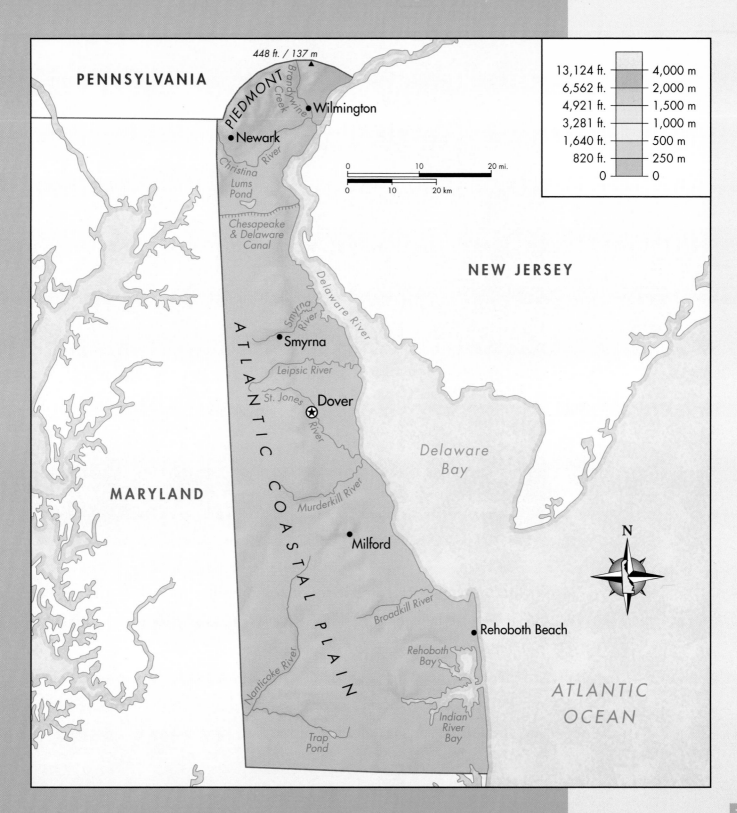

PENNSYLVANIA

448 ft. / 137 m

PIEDMONT

Brandywine Creek

• Wilmington

• Newark

Christina River

Lums Pond

Chesapeake & Delaware Canal

Delaware River

Smyrna River

• Smyrna

Leipsic River

St. Jones River

⊛ Dover

Delaware Bay

NEW JERSEY

ATLANTIC COASTAL PLAIN

Murderkill River

MARYLAND

• Milford

Broadkill River

Rehoboth Bay

Nanticoke River

• Rehoboth Beach

Indian River Bay

Trap Pond

ATLANTIC OCEAN

N

13,124 ft.	4,000 m
6,562 ft.	2,000 m
4,921 ft.	1,500 m
3,281 ft.	1,000 m
1,640 ft.	500 m
820 ft.	250 m
0	0

0   10   20 mi.

0   10   20 km

Soybeans are one of Delaware's most important farm products.

Piedmont. This area is made up of rolling hills and rich fertile valleys. Delaware's highest point of 447.85 feet (136.5 m) is located in the Piedmont Plateau.

Much of the state is ideal for farming. Farmers in Delaware grow mostly corn and soybeans. They also grow lots of fruits and vegetables, such as peas, asparagus, and tomatoes.

Despite its small size, Delaware has an abundance of plant and animal life. Many trees are native to Delaware, such as yellow poplars, pines, oaks, cedars, sycamores, and beeches. One of the country's largest stands of bald cypress trees is located in southern Delaware. During the Christmas season, people make wreaths from Delaware's state tree, the American Holly.

Colorful flowers and plants blanket Delaware from spring until the first frost. Orchids, water lilies, honeysuckle, and violets are just a few of the many plants native to the region. Magnolias and pink lady's slippers bloom in swampy areas. Delaware is also known for its sweet and juicy blueberries and cranberries.

Delaware's location on the Atlantic Coast makes it the perfect nesting and feeding ground for birds. Snowy egrets, hawks, sandpipers, blue herons, and cardinals all make their home in Delaware. Many of these birds feast on Delaware's large supply of fish, shellfish, and other water-dwelling creatures. The largest population of horseshoe crabs in the world lives in Delaware. The eggs of horseshoe crabs make a delicious meal for plovers. The state fish is the weak-

Pink lady's slippers can be found in parts of Delaware.

FIND OUT MORE

Many scientists worry about the shrinking number of horseshoe crabs in Delaware. What might be causing the state's population of horseshoe crabs to decline? What is Delaware doing to protect horseshoe crabs?

Delaware Bay is the world's largest spawning ground for horseshoe crabs.

fish, which lives in shallow ocean water. Crabs, clams, and bass also swim in Delaware's waters.

White-tailed deer and smaller mammals, such as muskrats, foxes, and raccoons, also make Delaware their home. The copperhead, a poisonous snake, can be found in Delaware. Sometimes whales and porpoises are spotted along the coast.

WATERWAYS

The Delaware River is the largest river in Delaware. It is also one of the most important trade routes in the United States. The only river that moves more products around the country is the Mississippi River.

The Delaware River is the longest free-flowing river in the eastern United States.

Most winter precipitation falls as rain, but snow covers the ground occasionally.

The Delaware begins its long 300-mile (483-km) journey to Delaware Bay in southern New York. As it makes its way southward to the sea, the river forms the boundary between Delaware and New Jersey, New York and Pennsylvania, and Pennsylvania and New Jersey. Smaller rivers join the Delaware, such as the Christina, Appoquinimink, Smyrna, and Leipsic rivers.

There are more than fifty freshwater lakes and ponds in Delaware. Some of the largest are Lums Pond in northern Delaware and Trap Pond in southern Delaware. There are also several freshwater wetlands.

CLIMATE

Delaware has a very mild, wet climate. The Atlantic Ocean keeps it from getting too hot or too cold.

Along the shore, the climate is cooler in summer and warmer in winter than it is inland. The state's average summer temperature is about 85.6° Fahrenheit (30° Celsius). In winter the temperature can reach as high as 42°F (6°C). Delaware gets plenty of rain and snow. About 46 inches (117 centimeters) of precipitation falls each year.

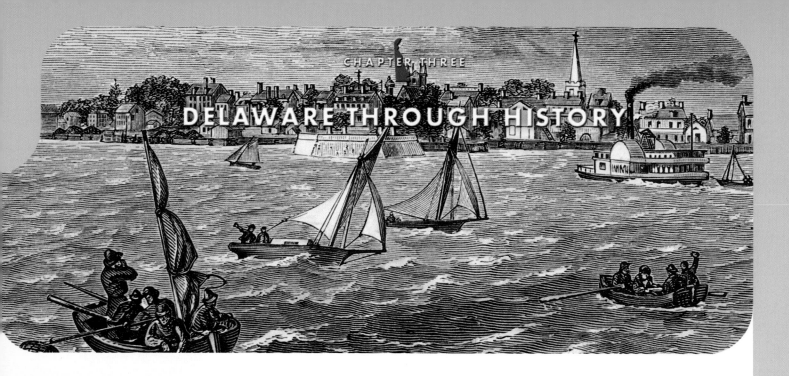

CHAPTER THREE

DELAWARE THROUGH HISTORY

New Castle was a bustling riverfront community in the late 1800s.

The first people came to what is now Delaware thousands of years ago. Scientists have uncovered bones, tools, and bowls more than 1,500 years old in Delaware. Before the first European settlers arrived, two tribes of Algonquin people lived in Delaware—the Lenni-Lenape in the north and the Nanticoke in the south.

The Lenni-Lenape are one of the oldest Native American nations in the Americas. Their name means "original people." Other Native American tribes call the Lenape "grandfather," in honor of their ancient heritage. They wrote the oldest history book in North America, called the *Walam Olum*, or Red Score (or Red Record).

The Nanticoke (whose name means "people of the tide water") once controlled all of the Delmarva Peninsula. A small

EXTRA! EXTRA!

In 1992, scientists uncovered several fossils near Smyrna, including whale, rhinoceros, and porpoise bones. They even found teeth from an 18-million-year-old chalicothere, an ancient ancestor of the horse that has long been extinct.

group lived along the Nanticoke River, but most of the Nanticoke lived along the eastern banks of the Chesapeake Bay. They were known for making beautiful beads.

These Native American groups lived in wigwams, or dome-shaped houses made of young tree branches covered with animal skins. The women grew corn, beans, and squash, and the men fished and hunted. Throughout the year, they held ceremonies to honor their gods. One important ceremony was the corn dance, held every spring. It honored the corn spirit, or Corn Mother, whom they believed protected their crops. These ancient rituals brought family members together and attracted huge crowds.

Native Americans spot Henry Hudson's ship, the *Half-Moon*, sailing into Delaware Bay.

EUROPEAN EXPLORERS ARRIVE

Henry Hudson, an Englishman, was the first known European to reach what is now Delaware. Hudson was hired by the Dutch to find a trade route from Europe to China. In 1609, Hudson and his crew sailed into what is now Delaware Bay. Hudson recalled seeing "a white sandy shore and within it green trees."

FIND OUT MORE

Henry Hudson made four voyages to North America. He explored three North American waterways that are named after him: the Hudson River, the Hudson Bay, and Hudson Strait. Locate these waterways on a map of North America.

English sea captain Samuel Argall followed Hudson in 1610. Argall sailed into the bay by accident on his way to Virginia from England. Argall named the bay De La Warr in honor of the first governor of Virginia, Lord De La Warr. It wasn't long before the Europeans began calling the Lenni-Lenape by a new name—the Delaware. They also gave the same name to the river that flowed into the bay, and to the bay's western shore.

In 1631 the first group of Dutch settlers arrived in what is now Lewes. They hoped to make money by farming and trading with the Native Americans. They built a sturdy wooden fort and named their settlement Zwaanendael, which means "valley of the swans." At first, the Dutch settlers had trouble getting along with Native Americans. When a misunderstanding arose in 1632, Native Americans destroyed the settlement.

The two groups were not always fighting, however. Native Americans taught the settlers how to grow food and hunt animals, which helped the settlers to survive. Unfortunately, when more settlers came to the Americas, Native Americans were forced from their homes to make room for them. The Europeans also brought deadly diseases, such as smallpox, which killed thousands of Native Americans. By 1690, few Native Americans still lived in Delaware.

NEW SWEDEN

The first permanent European settlement in Delaware was established in 1638. Thirty people from Sweden arrived aboard two ships named the *Kalmar Nyckel* and the *Vogel Grip*. They landed along a river they named Christina after their young queen. They moved to what is now Wilmington, and named their colony New Sweden. For a time, the settlers prospered by trading beaver pelts and other furs with the Native Americans. They set up churches and schools, and a fort called Fort Christina. They raised animals and grew corn.

A Swedish expedition, under the direction of Peter Minuit, landed in the Delaware area in 1638.

Soon, however, a fierce competition arose between the Dutch and the Swedes. The Dutch claimed land north of the Delaware River, called New Netherland. Both the Swedes and the Dutch wanted to control trade with Native Americans along the river. In 1655 the Dutch sent soldiers to New Sweden, and the town surrendered without a fight. The Dutch renamed the town New Amstel (now New Castle).

The Dutch and the Swedes weren't the only people making a living from the Delaware River. Fierce pirates roamed Delaware Bay, hunting for treasure among the many ships crossing the Atlantic. In 1698,

pirates attacked the town of Lewes and stole money and goods from the townspeople. According to legend, pirate treasures are still buried in the beaches near Cape Henlopen.

Pirates may have buried stolen treasures along the Delaware River.

ENGLAND TAKES OVER

In 1664 a fleet of English warships captured New Netherland, making the region part of the colony of New York. The Dutch recaptured the area in 1673, but returned it peacefully to the English the next year.

In 1682 Delaware became part of another English colony, Pennsylvania. The leader of Pennsylvania, William Penn, wanted to establish a route between his colony and the Atlantic Ocean. Because Delaware was south of Pennsylvania, the region became known as the Three Lower Counties of Pennsylvania, named New Castle, Kent, and Sussex.

Maryland also claimed land in the Three Lower Counties. For years, local armies and tax collectors from Maryland harassed the colonists living there. The dispute between Maryland and Pennsylva-

FIND OUT MORE

Today, Delaware is still divided into three counties: New Castle, Kent, and Sussex. It is the only state in which counties are subdivided into areas called hundreds. A hundred may include one or more towns, as well as surrounding rural areas. Why are these areas called hundreds?

nia was finally settled when two English surveyors, Charles Mason and Jeremiah Dixon, marked Delaware's southern and western boundaries in 1765. This boundary later became part of the Mason-Dixon Line, which still divides the North and South today.

Despite such problems, more people began settling in Delaware. Newark was founded in the early 1700s, and Dover was established in 1717. Many of the people who settled in Delaware were English Quakers, a peaceful religious group led by William Penn. In the 1730s, they helped settle the town of Wilmington near the site of Fort Christina.

William Penn controlled Pennsylvania and Delaware for many years.

THE AMERICAN REVOLUTION

In the 1760s and 1770s, the peaceful relationship between England and its colonies was nearing an end. England's King George III passed several unpopular taxes, which forced colonists to pay extra money to the English government when they bought certain goods, such as paper products or tea. The taxes angered many colonists. Sometimes they refused to pay the taxes. As time went by, the colonists became increasingly dissatisfied with British (English) rule.

In 1774 and 1775 the colonies held meetings in Philadelphia to discuss the problems between England and the colonies. These meetings were called the First and Second Continental Congress. Every colony sent delegates, or representatives. Delaware sent three delegates—Caesar

WHO'S WHO IN DELAWARE?

John Dickinson (1732–1808) was born in Maryland and grew up in Dover. During the Revolutionary War, he wrote so many papers arguing against English taxes that he became known as the Penman of the Revolution. He later served as governor ("president") of Delaware and Pennsylvania.

Rodney, Thomas McKean, and George Read.

In April 1775 the British army fired on colonial soldiers at Lexington and Concord in Massachusetts. They were the first battles of the Revolutionary War (also called the American Revolution, 1775–1783) between England and her colonies. At the Second Continental Congress, a vote was taken to decide whether or not the colonies should form a new country separate from England. Delaware's delegates could not agree. Thomas McKean and Caesar Rodney wanted to declare independence from England, but George Read did not. A vote for independence would require two of Delaware's delegates to vote in favor of it.

On voting day, July 2, 1776, Caesar Rodney was in Dover. When Rodney received word that the vote was being cast, he set out on horseback as fast as he could toward Philadelphia. Even though he was sick, Rodney rode 80 miles (129 km) in the driving rain, arriving just in time to cast the deciding vote in favor of independence.

On July 4, 1776, the delegates of the Second Continental Congress issued a document called the Declaration of Independence. This important document stated why the colonies wanted independence from England. By signing the declaration, the thirteen English colonies became the United States. "We must all hang together," the famous statesman Benjamin Franklin told his fellow delegates, "or most assuredly we shall all hang separately." In August of that year, Delaware became the first colony to call itself a state.

Despite its small size, Delaware was so valuable during the war that Thomas Jefferson, author of the Declaration of Independence, called it the Diamond State after the precious stone. Soldiers from Delaware fought so hard during the war that they earned the unusual nickname,

This painting by John Trumbull is titled "Signing of the Declaration of Independence."

FAMOUS FIRSTS

- Swedes built the first log cabins in North America near the mouth of the Delaware River in 1638
- The United States flag was first flown during the Battle of Cooch's Bridge in 1777
- The nation's first oceangoing iron steamboat, the *Bangor*, launched from Wilmington in 1844
- Christmas seals (stamps used to close a letter or package) were first sold at the Wilmington Post Office in 1907; they were designed by Emily P. Bissell, a Delaware author
- The country's first beauty contest was held at Rehoboth Beach in 1880; the winner received the title of "Miss United States"

"Blue Hen's Chickens," after the Delaware gamecocks prized for their fighting abilities. Some say that Delaware soldiers actually carried these fighting birds into battle. The soldiers yelled, "We're sons of the Blue Hen, and we're game to the end!"

The only battle fought in Delaware was the Battle of Cooch's Bridge on September 3, 1777. The British won the battle, but for three days, colonial troops held off British forces near Newark. Although they lost the Battle of Cooch's Bridge, soldiers from Delaware helped to win many battles in other colonies. After eight long years, the colonies won independence from Britain in September of 1783.

THE FIRST STATE

After the war ended, the new nation's leaders faced the difficult challenge of creating their own government. In 1787, America's leaders met in Philadelphia to discuss the issue. After many debates, they wrote the United States Constitution, a document that established the foundation of our government. On December 7, 1787, Delaware became the first state to ratify (approve) the Constitution. Ever since that day,

The Brandywine Creek was an important industrial area in Delaware. Flour mills, gunpowder mills, and paper mills were just a few of the businesses that sprang up along the river.

Delaware has been known as the "First State." In 1797, Delaware set up its own state government by writing a state constitution.

After the war, Delaware's economy boomed. Its natural harbors and central location along the Atlantic Coast made it an ideal place for shipping and trade. Many people with exciting new ideas came to Delaware. In 1785, Oliver Evans of Newport invented a machine that milled flour faster and easier than ever before. Jacob Broome built a cotton mill on Brandywine Creek, not far from Wilmington, in 1795. In 1802 a French immigrant named Eleuthère Irénée (E.I.) du Pont started a gunpowder mill on Brandywine Creek.

As more people came to Delaware, transportation improved. Several steamboat companies began taking passengers up and down the

Delaware River. In 1829, workers dug a waterway between the Delaware River and the Chesapeake Bay called the Chesapeake and Delaware (C&D) Canal. The canal created a shortcut between Philadelphia and Baltimore and made it easier to move people and goods across the region. Ships carrying lumber, grain, farm products, fish, and cotton could now sail directly through Delaware's New Castle County.

Steamboats carried products up the Delaware River to Philadelphia.

Another exciting new development in transportation was the railroad. In 1831 the New Castle and Frenchtown Railroad was completed, connecting northern and southern Delaware. The railroad didn't just help people to travel faster—it also helped farmers in central and southern Delaware get their crops to market quicker than ever before.

THE CIVIL WAR

Peace did not last long in the new nation. In 1861, the country was torn apart by the worst crisis in its history—the Civil War (1861–1865). One of the causes of the war was disagreement between the North and South about slavery. Slavery began in the United States in the 1600s, when Europeans captured people from the west coast of Africa and sold them to American colonists.

The colonists forced slaves to perform hard labor on farms. Slaveowners treated their slaves like property. Slaves were not paid for their work. They could not travel, and they were not allowed to learn how to read or write.

By 1860, at least four million slaves lived in the United States. Most slaves lived in the South where they labored on large rice and cotton farms called plantations. Southern plantation owners depended on slaves to plant and harvest their crops. They thought they could not survive without slaves.

A smaller number of slaves also lived in northern cities, such as Boston, Philadelphia, and New York, but most people in the North worked in factories or shops for wages. Although slavery was legal in Delaware, few slaves lived there. By 1861, there were fewer than 2,000 slaves and more than 18,000 free African-Americans living in Delaware.

After the Revolutionary War, many people in the North began to think that slavery was wrong, and they spoke out against it. These people were called abolitionists because they wanted to abolish, or end, slavery.

Some people helped slaves escape to freedom on the Underground Railroad. The Underground Railroad wasn't really a railroad at all. Instead, it was a secret chain of people and places where slaves could

Many African-Americans escaped from the South and began new lives elsewhere.

find safety on their dangerous journey north. The safe houses were called stations, and slaves who traveled from station to station were called passengers. The people who led the slaves to freedom were called conductors.

For many slaves, the last station before reaching freedom was the home of Thomas Garrett, a Quaker merchant who lived in Wilmington. Garrett helped more than 2,000 slaves escape from the South. When a court fined Garrett so heavily that he lost all his property, Garrett stood firm in his beliefs. He told the court, "I say to thee and to all in this court room, that if anyone knows a fugitive who wants shelter . . . send him to Thomas Garrett, and he will befriend him."

As new territories entered the United States, tensions between the northern and southern states erupted. Lawmakers in the North worked hard to keep slavery out of the new states, which angered many people in the South. In 1861, eleven slave states seceded, or withdrew, from the United

FIND OUT MORE

Pretend you are a young slave forced to work on a plantation. Write a journal and tell about your life. What food do you eat? What clothes do you wear? Do you go to school? What kind of work do you do?

WHAT'S IN A NAME?

Many names of places in Delaware have interesting origins.

Name	Comes From or Means
Delaware	Lord De La Warr, governor of Virginia
Delmar and Marydel	A combination of the words Delaware and Maryland
Christina River, Fort Christina	Christina, Queen of Sweden
Pea Patch Island	From a tall tale about a boat carrying peas that sank in the Delaware River
Rehoboth	Biblical term meaning "wide spaces"
Zwaanendael	Dutch word meaning "valley of the swans"

States and formed the Confederate States of America. Shortly after the southern states left the Union, the Civil War began.

Delaware had many ties to the North and decided to remain in the Union. Between 13,000 and 14,000 young men from Delaware joined the Union army. But not everyone in Delaware supported the Union. Several hundred young men left Delaware to fight for the Confederates. Anyone caught helping the Confederate army in Delaware was sent to Fort Delaware, a terrible prisoner-of-war camp on Pea Patch Island. At one time, Fort Delaware held more than 12,500 prisoners.

Although no major battles were fought in Delaware, its industries helped the Union army. The DuPont Company produced more than a third of the Union's gunpowder. Shipyards in Wilmington built many of the Union's naval vessels.

When the North won the war in 1865, the United States government outlawed slavery. The few remaining slaves who lived in Delaware were set free. The former Confederate states were allowed back into the Union in 1870, but it would take many years to rebuild the battered South, where much of the war was fought. It would be even longer before former slaves were treated equally under the law.

At the turn of the century, Delaware's population boomed. Thousands of people from Europe came to work in Delaware's thriving industries, such as shipbuilding and gunpowder manufacturing. By 1910 there were more than 200,000 people living in Delaware.

After the Civil War, life improved for some people. In 1904, the state of Delaware officially recognized the Nanticoke people. Until then, most people thought that the Nanticoke had disappeared from Delaware more than two hundred years earlier. Scientists and teachers came to Delaware to learn all they could about the Nanticoke culture.

Women began to stand up for their rights, too. At this time, only men could vote, and many women in Delaware fought hard to change

This photograph shows a view of Main Street in Dover in 1913.

that. In 1917, Delawareans Florence Bayard Hilles and Mabel Vernon joined thousands of women from other states in a march on Washington, D.C., demanding the right to vote. They were arrested and jailed, but their hard work eventually paid off. In 1920, all American women won the right to vote.

It would take much longer, however, for African-Americans to see improvements. Throughout the late 1800s and early 1900s, Delaware was racially segregated, which meant that blacks and whites were kept separate by law. These "Jim Crow" laws forced African-Americans to attend different schools, eat at certain restaurants, and use separate entrances and waiting areas in public places. African-Americans were often denied jobs and educational opportunities that were open to white people.

Mabel Vernon devoted much of her life to women's rights.

HARD TIMES

In 1914 a war broke out in Europe known as World War I (1914–1918). Delaware's industries again played an important role in the war. Shipyards, gunpowder mills, textile mills, and other businesses in Delaware worked at full capacity to help the British and French armies. In 1917 the United States joined the war, and about 10,000 people from Delaware joined the armed forces.

EXTRA! EXTRA!

Cecile Steele of Ocean View, Delaware started the broiler industry in 1923. After accidentally receiving 500 chickens instead of the 50 she originally ordered, Steele raised the chickens until they were 16 weeks old and sold them for a profit. This was the beginning of the modern poultry industry.

During the Great Depression, members of the Civilian Conservation Corps were hired by the government to build roads and parks through the soggy marshland in Delaware.

Delaware's economy began to fall apart in 1929. In October that year, the stock market crashed, and thousands of people across the country lost money that they had invested in businesses. As a result, many businesses closed, including banks and factories. Thousands of people in Delaware lost their jobs and homes. Without jobs, many people could no longer afford to buy things they needed, such as food and clothing. This period is known as the Great Depression (1929–1939). The United States government tried to help people by giving them jobs building roads and public parks, but jobs remained scarce.

In 1939, another war erupted in Europe. People in the United States wanted to stay out of World War II (1939–1945), but that soon proved impossible. On December 8, 1941, Japan bombed a United States naval base at Pearl Harbor in Hawaii, and the United States declared war.

The war helped to end the Great Depression. In Delaware, factories began operating at full speed once again to help the war effort. In 1938, the DuPont Company introduced nylon, which was used to make parachutes. The company soon became the state's biggest employer.

After the war, giant corporations moved to Delaware, such as Chrysler, General Foods, and General Motors, in part because taxes were so low. While industries thrived in northern Delaware's cities, agriculture boomed in southern Delaware, thanks to improvements in transportation and agricultural methods. Sussex County became one of the most important farming areas in the country. By the 1950s, farmers in Delaware were raising one-fourth of the nation's broiler chickens.

DuPont chemist Wallace Carothers stretches a piece of nylon, which he invented in 1937.

MAKING PROGRESS

In the 1950s, life began to improve for African-Americans in Delaware. In 1950, African-Americans were allowed unlimited admission into the University of Delaware for the first time. Thirteen years later, the state legislature (Delaware's lawmaking body), passed a bill banning segregation in public restaurants. In 1969 the legislature approved a bill ending discrimination in the rental or sale of housing in Delaware. Several years later, communities began busing African-American children to white school districts in an effort to integrate blacks and whites.

MODERN TIMES

As Delaware continued to grow, problems arose. In the 1960s, people in Delaware began to worry about the growing problem of pollution. There was no way to track how much pollution Delaware's factories produced, and the state's water and air were becoming filthy. In 1969, state lawmakers set up the Department of Natural Resources and Environmental Control to manage air and water pollution in Delaware. In 1971 the state legislature passed the Coastal Zone Act to help clean up the Delaware River. To this day, the act prevents businesses from building factories on Delaware's coastline.

In the 1970s the United States economy began to slow down. In Delaware, many people lost their jobs and homes. To attract

FIND OUT MORE

Pretend that you are a state lawmaker in Delaware who is concerned about the environment. What might you do to help clean up and protect the environment? How would you gain support for your ideas?

more businesses to Delaware, the state government lowered taxes, which meant that businesses had to give less of their money to the government. The plan worked. By 1989, many companies had moved their headquarters to Delaware. These businesses help make Delaware one of the richest states in the country.

More people also began visiting Delaware's beautiful beaches. In 1998, tourists (visitors) spent more than $342 million in Sussex

Wilmington's many businesses attract workers from the nearby states of New Jersey, Pennsylvania, and Maryland.

County. Rehoboth Beach is so popular with people from Washington D.C., that it has become known as the "Nation's Summer Capital."

Today, our country's first state is ready for the twenty-first century. In November of 2000, Delaware elected its first female governor, Ruth Ann Minner. It's just one of the many ways the people of Delaware are preparing to meet the challenges that lie ahead.

CHAPTER FOUR

GOVERNING DELAWARE

Delaware declared itself a state in 1776, shortly after the signing of the Declaration of Independence. It also established a state government separate from Pennsylvania and wrote a state constitution. (Delaware's statehood became official in 1787, when it was the first state to ratify the United States Constitution.) A constitution is an official document that tells how the state will be governed. The first state constitution was created in 1776, and it was later rewritten in 1797. The current constitution has been in effect since 1897. It has been amended, or changed, more than 100 times. Delaware is the only state that can change its constitution without the approval of voters.

Delaware's government is organized in a way similar to the United States government. It divides the power among three branches, or parts: the legislative, the executive, and the judicial. These three branches work together to govern the state.

Legislative Hall is the center of Delaware's government.

EXECUTIVE BRANCH

The executive branch makes sure that Delaware's laws are carried out and enforced. The governor is head of the executive branch. He or she is elected by the people of Delaware. The governor appoints a secretary of state, judges, and members of the board of education. The governor is elected every four years, and may be reelected only once. Other elected officials in the executive branch include the lieutenant governor, the attorney general, the state treasurer, the auditor of accounts, and the insurance commissioner.

LEGISLATIVE BRANCH

The legislative branch makes laws for the state. In Delaware, the legislative branch is called the general assembly. The people of Delaware elect lawmakers, called legislators, who serve in this branch of government.

The general assembly is made up of two parts: an upper house and a lower house. The upper house is called the senate. People who serve in the senate are called senators. The lower house is the house of representatives; its members are called representatives. The lieutenant governor

serves as president of the senate. Together, these groups vote on the passage of new laws for the state of Delaware. The president casts a vote only in the event that a tiebreaker is necessary.

There are 21 senators and 41 representatives in Delaware's general assembly. Senators serve four-year terms, and representatives serve two-year terms. There is no limit to the number of times that representatives and senators may be reelected.

Delaware's lawmakers meet inside Legislative Hall.

JUDICIAL BRANCH

The judicial branch interprets, or explains, the state's laws through the court system. There are several types of courts in Delaware that hear different kinds of cases. The state's highest, or most important court, is the state supreme court. It is made up of one chief justice (judge) and four associate justices. The supreme court determines if lower court rulings are fair. It also supervises the entire court system of Delaware.

Below the supreme court is the superior court, which hears civil and criminal cases. When people or organizations feel that their rights have been violated, they may file a civil case. Criminal cases are those in which a crime has been committed, such as robbery. The superior court has 17 justices. It meets in all three of Delaware's counties.

Other courts are the court of chancery, family court, the court of common pleas, and the justice of the peace court. The court of chancery hears cases such as land disputes or contract-related issues. Family court hears matters such as divorce and child support. The justice of the peace court handles civil cases involving less than $15,000, and the court of common pleas hears civil cases involving less than $50,000.

DELAWARE STATE GOVERNMENT

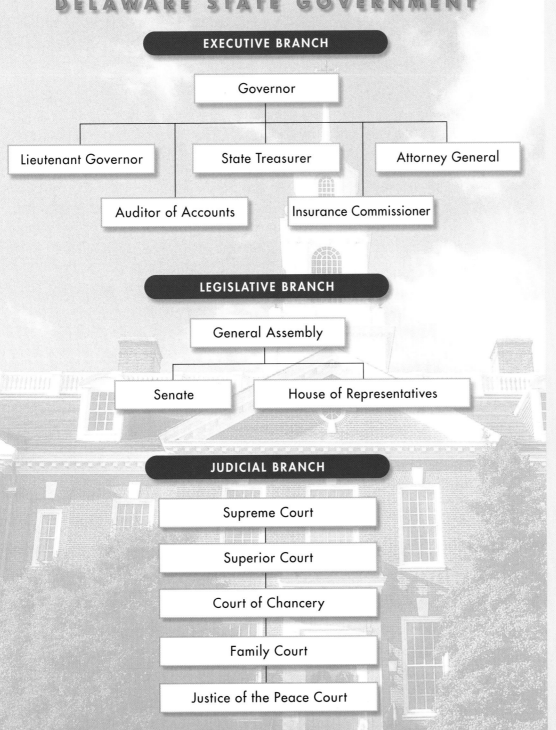

EXECUTIVE BRANCH

Governor

Lieutenant Governor

State Treasurer

Attorney General

Auditor of Accounts

Insurance Commissioner

LEGISLATIVE BRANCH

General Assembly

Senate

House of Representatives

JUDICIAL BRANCH

Supreme Court

Superior Court

Court of Chancery

Family Court

Justice of the Peace Court

DELAWARE GOVERNORS

Name	Term	Name	Term
*John McKinly	1777	William H. Ross	1851–1855
*Thomas McKean	1777	Peter F. Causey	1855–1859
*George Read	1777–1778	William Burton	1859–1863
*Caesar Rodney	1778–1781	William Cannon	1863–1865
*John Dickinson	1781–1782	Gove Saulsbury	1865–1871
*John Cook	1782–1783	James Ponder	1871–1875
*Nicholas Van Dyke	1783–1786	John P. Cochran	1875–1879
*Thomas Collins	1786–1789	John W. Hall	1879–1883
*Jehu Davis	1789	Charles C. Stockley	1883–1887
*Joshua Clayton	1789–1793	Benjamin T. Biggs	1887–1891
Joshua Clayton	1793–1796	Robert J. Reynolds	1891–1895
Gunning Bedford, Sr.	1796–1797	Joshua H. Marvil	1895
Daniel Rogers	1797–1799	William T. Watson	1895–1897
Richard Bassett	1799–1801	Ebe T. Tunnell	1897–1901
James Sykes	1801–1802	John Hunn	1901–1905
David Hall	1802–1805	Preston Lea	1905–1909
Nathaniel Mitchell	1805–1808	Simon S. Pennewill	1909–1913
George Truitt	1808–1811	Charles R. Miller	1913–1917
Joseph Haslet	1811–1814	John G. Townsend, Jr.	1917–1921
Daniel Rodney	1814–1817	William D. Denney	1921–1925
John Clark	1817–1820	Robert P. Robinson	1925–1929
Jacob Stout	1820–1821	C. Douglass Buck	1929–1937
John Collins	1821–1822	Richard C. McMullen	1937–1941
Caleb Rodney	1822–1823	Walter W. Bacon	1941–1949
Joseph Haslet	1823	Elbert N. Carvel	1949–1953
Charles Thomas	1823–1824	J. Caleb Boggs	1953–1960
Samuel Paynter	1824–1827	David Buckson	1960–1961
Charles Polk	1827–1830	Elbert N. Carvel	1961–1965
David Hazzard	1830–1833	Charles L. Terry, Jr.	1965–1969
Caleb P. Bennett	1833–1836	Russell W. Peterson	1969–1973
Charles Polk	1836–1837	Sherman W. Tribbitt	1973–1977
Cornelius P. Comegys	1837–1841	Pierre S. du Pont IV	1977–1985
William B. Cooper	1841–1845	Michael N. Castle	1985–1993
Thomas Stockton	1845–1846	Dale E. Wolf	1993
Joseph Maull	1846	Thomas R. Carper	1993–2000
William Temple	1846–1847	Ruth A. Minner	2000–
William Tharp	1847–1851	*Until 1793, Delaware's chief executive was called president	

The judicial branch is the only branch of government whose members are not elected by the people. The governor appoints all judges, with the approval of the state senate. Each judge serves for 12 years.

TAKE A TOUR OF DOVER, DELAWARE'S STATE CAPITAL

Dover is the state capital of Delaware. It is also the state's second largest city and home to many thriving businesses. More than 30,000 people live in Dover.

One of the highlights of Dover is the capitol building, called Legislative Hall. The capitol is home to Delaware's lawmakers; the legislature meets on the first floor. Built in 1933, it is one of the country's newest state capitols.

One of the country's oldest capitol buildings is also in Dover. Before Legislative Hall was built, Delaware's lawmakers met in the Old State House, built in 1792. Today, the Old State House is a museum which includes a restored

Delaware's lawmakers used to meet in the senate chambers of the Old State House.

A stone statue of Caesar Rodney commemorates his famous ride.

courtroom from the 1700s and exhibits about Delaware history.

The Old State House is located on a historic park called the Green. The Green was Dover's first downtown area, where the people of Delaware heard a reading of the Declaration of Independence in 1776. A stone statue of Revolutionary War hero Caesar Rodney stands on the Green in the cemetery of Christ Episcopal Church. Nearby Constitution Park has a 4-foot (1.2-m) stone cube inscribed with the United States Constitution.

One block west of the Green is the Delaware Archaeology Museum and the Museum of Small Town Life. The Archaeology Museum displays ancient objects from a Native American burial ground. The Museum of Small Town Life shows visitors what life was like in Delaware in the early 1900s. It includes a general store, a post office, and a woodworking shop.

Behind the Delaware Archaeology Museum is the Delaware State Museum, which documents the state's political history. If you like music, take a tour of the Johnson Victrola Museum, part of the Delaware State Museum. It is a tribute to Delaware native Eldridge Johnson, who helped to develop the first record player called a Victrola. At the museum you can listen to records from the 1920s played on a Victrola.

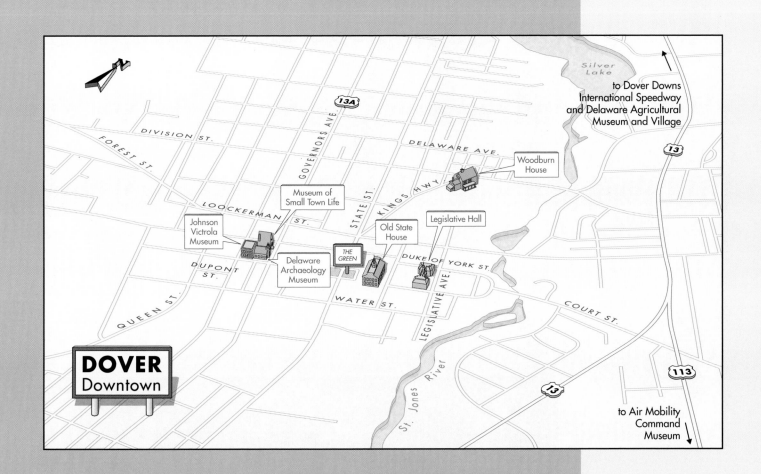

Silver Lake

13A

DIVISION ST.

FOREST ST.

DELAWARE AVE.

to Dover Downs
International Speedway
and Delaware Agricultural
Museum and Village

13

Woodburn
House

LOOCKERMAN ST.

Museum of
Small Town Life

GOVERNORS AVE.

STATE ST.

KINGS HWY.

Johnson
Victrola
Museum

THE
GREEN

Old State
House

Legislative Hall

DUPONT ST.

Delaware
Archaeology
Museum

DUKE OF YORK ST.

QUEEN ST.

WATER ST.

LEGISLATIVE AVE.

COURT ST.

DOVER
Downtown

St. Jones River

113

13

to Air Mobility
Command
Museum

Several historic houses are located in downtown Dover. Woodburn House, the official home of the state governor, was once a station on the Underground Railroad. Cannon House, built in 1862, was home to noted astronomer Annie Jump Cannon.

Head east of downtown Dover and visit the Air Mobility Command Museum at Dover Air Force Base. Some of the country's largest cargo and fighter planes are displayed there. The biggest plane is called the C-5 Galaxy. It's almost as long as a football field, and can hold about 100 cars.

The C-5 Galaxy is used to deliver supplies, including tanks and helicopters, to places all over the world.

If you want to learn about the history of Delaware farmers, take a trip to the Delaware Agricultural Museum and Village. This museum traces two hundred years of farm life. Behind the main building is a recreation of an 1890s village. There's even a log cabin from the 1600s.

Dover is also a great place for racing fans. The NASCAR "monster car" races at Dover Downs International Speedway draw more than 100,000 fans to Dover every spring and fall. In the off-season, harness horse racing takes place at the speedway.

CHAPTER FIVE

THE PEOPLE AND PLACES OF DELAWARE

A group of fishermen wait anxiously for the next boat trip in Lewes.

According to 2000 census figures, 783,600 people live in the First State. Most people live in cities or suburban areas. About two of every three people in Delaware live in or around Wilmington, the state's largest city. Most of the state's industries and businesses are located in the Wilmington area.

Today, most Delawareans were born in the United States. Almost 8 out of every 10 people are of European descent. About 20 of every 100 people are African-American, and 5 of every 100 are Hispanic or Latino. Asians, Native Americans, and people of other races make up the rest of the state's population.

Religion is important to many people in Delaware. The first Methodist Episco-

EXTRA! EXTRA!

Outside of Dover is a small Amish community. The Amish came to North America from Switzerland in the 1690s. They choose to live a simple life with few modern conveniences, such as televisions and radios. To earn money, they sell fresh produce, baked goods, and handcrafted furniture at markets in the Dover area.

pal Church in America was established in Delaware in 1784. Today, the largest religious denomination in the state is the Roman Catholic Church. The state is also home to Baptists, Episcopalians, Lutherans, and Presbyterians. Other Delawareans are Jewish, Methodist, Muslim, or Jehovah's Witnesses.

EDUCATION

Education is also important to the people of Delaware. The state's public school system was established in 1829. Today, all children in Delaware between the ages of five and fifteen must go to school. The majority of children attend public schools, but many go to private or religious schools or are schooled at home.

The University of Delaware in Newark is the state's largest public college. Other Delaware colleges are Goldey-Beacom College, Widener University School of Law, Wilmington College, and Delaware State University. The state also has several community and technical colleges.

WHO'S WHO IN DELAWARE?

Richard Allen (1760–1831) was born a slave in Philadelphia and grew up on a plantation in Delaware. He saved enough money to buy his freedom in 1786, then moved back to Philadelphia. In 1816, he founded the African Methodist Episcopal Church (A.M.E.), the first African-American religious denomination in the United States.

The University of Delaware, founded in 1743, now has almost 20,000 students in attendance.

Delaware may be a small state, but it is very wealthy. In April 2000, *Governing* magazine rated Delaware's economy the strongest in the nation. Most people in Delaware work in service industries. These are businesses, such as law firms, banks, hotels, or hospitals, that provide services to groups or individuals. Most of these industries are located in the Wilmington area, home to about 173,000 corporations. In southern

A chemist works in a laboratory at DuPont.

Delaware, many people work in seaside resort towns such as Rehoboth, Dewey, and Bethany beaches.

Manufacturing is also a vital part of Delaware's economy. The chemical industry employs the largest number of people. The DuPont Company in Wilmington is the biggest company in Delaware. It manufactures the chemicals used to make nylon, dyes, medicines, and plastics.

Some manufacturing businesses in Delaware make fabrics for clothing and furniture, while others make paper, rubber, and plastic products. In southern Delaware,

EXTRA! EXTRA!

ILC Dover is a company in Frederica that makes space suits. ILC made the first suit worn on the moon. It was used by Neil Armstrong for his famous 1969 moonwalk.

In Newark, assembly-line workers build cars for Daimler-Chrysler.

several companies process the food grown by Delaware's farmers. There are also large automobile factories in Newark and Newport.

At one time, most people in Delaware made a living by farming. Today, much of Delaware's land is still devoted to farming, but agriculture makes up only a small part of Delaware's economy. There are about 6,000 farms in Delaware. Most farmland is devoted to growing corn and soybeans. Other pro-

FIND OUT MORE

Delaware was once famous for its delicious peaches. That's why the state flower is the peach blossom. Today, Delaware's farmers don't grow as many peaches as they used to because most of the state's peach trees died. What caused the peach trees to die?

Broiler chickens feed at a poultry house in Sussex County.

duce includes fruits and vegetables such as peas, asparagus, tomatoes, and melons.

Most of the grain grown in Delaware is used to feed the state's huge broiler industry. Broiler chickens are Delaware's most important farm product. The state produces more than 225 million broiler chickens a year. That's about one chicken for every person in the United States!

Fishing also brings in money to the state. Commercial fishing boats and chartered boats near seaside towns such as Lewes catch saltwater fish in Delaware Bay and the Atlantic Ocean. Crabs are their most important catch, but they also fish for clams, sea bass, and carp.

Chicken is one of Delaware's most valuable agricultural products. This recipe for breaded chicken fingers is just one of many easy, delicious ways to prepare chicken. Remember to ask an adult for help!

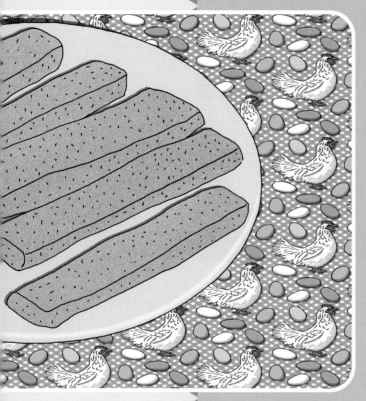

BREADED CHICKEN FINGERS

(serves 4)
4 skinless, boneless chicken breasts, cut into strips
1 egg, beaten
1 cup milk
1 cup all-purpose flour
1 cup dried breadcrumbs
1 teaspoon salt
1 teaspoon baking powder
vegetable oil

1. Place chicken in a large, resealable plastic bag.
2. In a small bowl, combine egg and milk.
3. Pour egg mixture into bag with chicken. Seal and shake. Refrigerate for one hour.
4. In another resealable plastic bag mix together flour, breadcrumbs, salt, and baking powder.
5. Remove chicken from refrigerator and drain.
6. Place chicken in flour mixture bag. Seal and shake to coat.
7. In a large skillet, heat oil.
8. Add chicken and fry in hot oil until golden brown, and juices run clear. Drain on paper towels and serve.

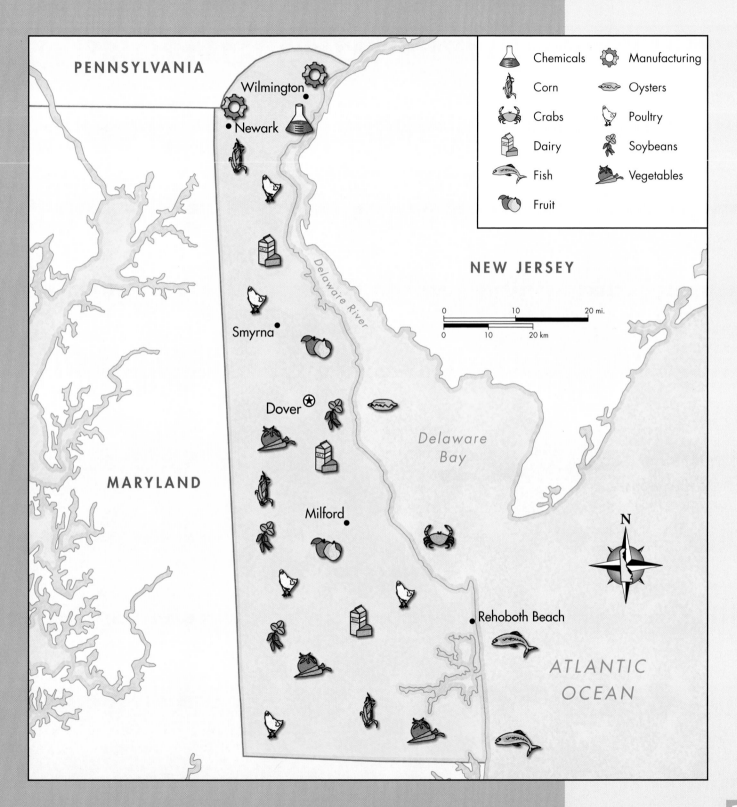

PENNSYLVANIA

Wilmington

Newark

MARYLAND

Smyrna

Dover ✪

Milford

Delaware River

NEW JERSEY

Delaware Bay

Rehoboth Beach

ATLANTIC OCEAN

Chemicals		Manufacturing
Corn		Oysters
Crabs		Poultry
Dairy		Soybeans
Fish		Vegetables
Fruit		

0   10   20 mi.
0   10   20 km

N

New Castle County

Let's start our tour in New Castle County, where there are lots of great things to see and do. At Fort Christina National Park in Wilmington, you can see a recreation of the *Kalmar Nyckel*, one of the ships that brought the first Swedish settlers to Delaware. Nearby is Old Swedes Church, built by Swedish settlers in 1698. It is the oldest Protestant church still in use in the United States today. Inside the church is a pipe organ with 913 pipes!

If you like music and theater, you'll love Wilmington. The Delaware Symphony performs classical music in the Grand Opera House, built in 1871. The Opera House is filled with beautiful fixtures, such as winding staircases and painted ceilings. Theatergoers can see plays at the Delaware Theatre Company's Little Theater on the Christina River. The Delaware Children's Theater presents plays based on fairy tales and other stories for children of all ages.

The Delaware Art Museum in Wilmington houses the works of Howard Pyle, Delaware's most famous artist. Pyle opened a school of art in Wilmington in

WHO'S WHO IN DELAWARE?

Howard Pyle (1853–1911) was one of the most successful illustrators of his time. He illustrated many popular children's books, including *The Merry Adventures of Robin Hood* and *The Story of King Arthur and His Knights*. He was born in Wilmington.

A replica of the *Kalmar Nyckel* is docked at the Port of Wilmington.

1900 while he was working as a writer and illustrator. He offered classes free of charge to talented students. The nearby USA Riverfront Arts Center showcases art from around the world.

The Delaware History Center tells the story of the First State. At Grandma's Attic in the museum's Discovery Center, you can dress up like the early settlers of Delaware, handle tools they used, and hear storytellers. A few doors down sits Old Town Hall, the center of many political and social activities in Wilmington during the 1800s.

Minor league baseball fans root for the state's professional baseball team, the Wilmington Blue Rocks, at Judy Johnson Field at Daniel S. Frawley Stadium. The stadium seats 5,900 fans. If baseball isn't your sport, check out the horse races at Delaware Park. This tree-lined park is about 5 miles (8 km) southwest of Wilmington.

To enjoy the outdoors you don't need to travel far from Wilmington. Bellevue State Park on the northeast edge of Wilmington has 270 acres (109 ha) of picnic grounds and nature trails. Southwest of Wilmington is Lums Pond State Park, which stretches along the Chesapeake and Delaware Canal. Lums Pond is Delaware's largest freshwater pond and home to many birds and animals. There, you can swim, fish, hike, or enjoy a boat ride.

North of Wilmington are the rolling hills of the Brandywine Valley. The Hagley Museum, one of Delaware's most popular museums, is located there. It's the original site where E. I. du Pont first began making gunpowder 200 years ago. You can learn how a water-powered gunpowder factory worked and how the factory's employees lived. The nearby

Winterthur Museum and Gardens was once the home of Henry Francis du Pont. The nine-story museum houses some of the world's finest antiques and decorative arts.

Let's travel about 7 miles (11 km) south of Wilmington to historic New Castle, Delaware's first capital. Many old homes and churches in

Lums Park, built around the largest freshwater pond in Delaware, is a great place for fishing, boating, and swimming.

A visit to Pea Patch Island takes you back to Civil War times. Fort Delaware dates back to 1859.

New Castle have been restored and are open to tourists. One of the most interesting buildings is the Old Court House, where the state's assembly met until 1777. Today, it is a museum that houses portraits of Delaware's founders and many historical artifacts.

About 16 miles (26 km) south of Wilmington, a ferry will take you from Delaware City to Pea Patch Island, where you can tour Fort Delaware, a famous Civil War prison camp. Every summer, people dressed as Confederate and Union soldiers give guided tours of the underground cells where prisoners were kept. If you're lucky, you may see a musket and cannon demonstration.

West of Wilmington is Newark, Delaware's third-largest city. Newark is home of the University of Delaware. It is also the site of the only Revolutionary War battle fought on Delaware soil, the Battle of Cooch's Bridge.

One of Newark's most popular attractions is the Iron Hill Museum of Natural History. You can see fossils of prehistoric animals that once

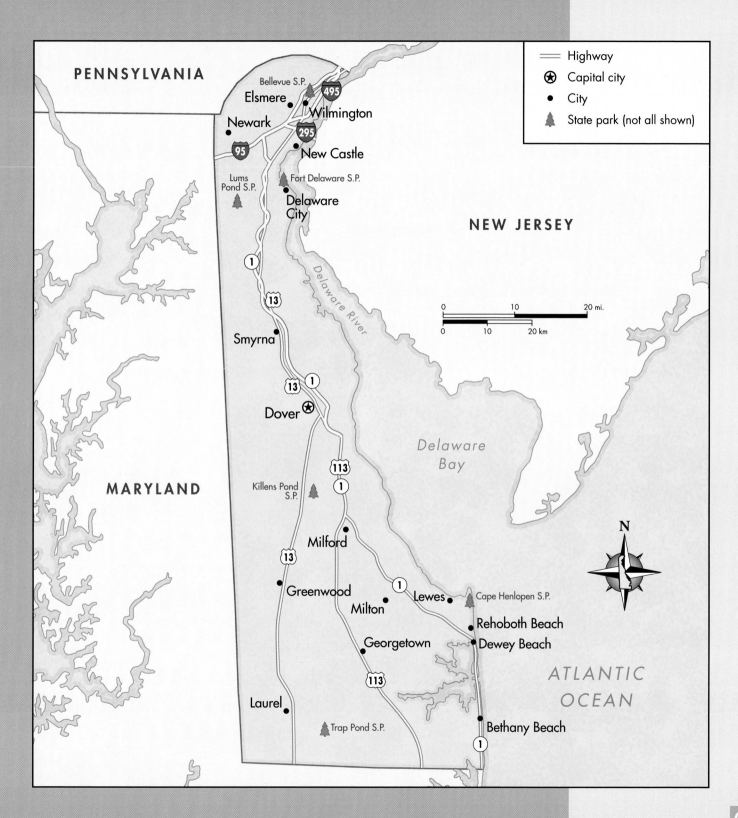

PENNSYLVANIA

Bellevue S.P.

Elsmere

Wilmington

Newark

495

295

New Castle

95

Fort Delaware S.P.

Lums
Pond S.P.

Delaware
City

NEW JERSEY

1

13

Smyrna

Delaware River

13 **1**

Dover

MARYLAND

Delaware
Bay

113

1

Killens Pond
S.P.

Milford

13

Greenwood

1

Lewes

Cape Henlepen S.P.

Milton

Rehoboth Beach

Georgetown

Dewey Beach

113

ATLANTIC
OCEAN

Laurel

Trap Pond S.P.

Bethany Beach

1

N

Highway

Capital city

City

State park (not all shown)

0   10   20 mi.

0   10   20 km

roamed Delaware. The museum even has the bones of a giant sea lizard called a mosasaur. The mosasaur lived 100 million years ago when Delaware was under water. The museum also shows how the Lenni-Lenape lived hundreds of years ago.

Kent County

Next, let's travel to Kent County and see the fully restored John Dickinson Plantation south of Dover. John Dickinson was a signer and writer of the United States Constitution, and a governor of Delaware. The plantation's original brick house was built in 1740, but was destroyed by fire in 1804. The house was rebuilt in 1896.

About 13 miles (21 km) south of Dover is Kent County's only state park, Killens Pond State Park. You can hike, fish, camp, bike, or throw horseshoes on its 1,040 acres (421 ha). There's also a pool with water slides.

Kent County is the perfect place for nature lovers. Just east of Dover, you can tour one of Delaware's hidden gems, the Bombay Hook National Wildlife Refuge. If you like to birdwatch, you're in luck—its 16,000 acres (6,475 ha) of preserved wetlands are a haven for hundreds of bird species including herons, ducks, egrets, and the occasional bald eagle. More than

Millions of snow geese winter at Bombay Hook National Wildlife Refuge.

130,000 snow geese flock to the Bombay Hook each year. It is one of the largest national wildlife refuges on the Atlantic Coast. Bowers Beach and nearby areas are prime sites for viewing the springtime mating and laying eggs of horseshoe crabs.

About 20 miles (32 km) south of Dover, visit the Prime Hook National Wildlife Refuge. There are plenty of birds there too, but you can also see red-bellied turtles, bullfrogs, and red-backed salamanders. If you like to canoe, there are more than 15 miles (24 km) of streams to explore.

Sussex County

Next, let's travel south to Sussex County. This part of Delaware is famous for its beautiful sandy beaches. During the summer months, tourists from all over the world travel to Rehoboth, Dewey, Bethany, and Fenwick Island beaches.

At Cape Henlopen State Park, there's biking, fishing, canoeing, and hiking. The park is also the home of the "walking dunes." They're called walking dunes because strong winds move them over time so that they shift position. An 80-foot (24-m) sand dune

Rehoboth Beach is one of Delaware's most popular tourist areas in the summer.

named the Great Dune is the highest sand dune between Cape Hatteras in North Carolina and Cape Cod in Massachusetts.

The Rehoboth Summer Children's Theatre presents plays all summer long, such as Snow White, Jack and the Beanstalk, and Cinderella. Every September, the town of Millsboro hosts the annual Nanticoke Indian Powwow. It's a 2-day festival of traditional Native American dancing and story telling.

In the seaside town of Lewes, take a tour of the Zwaanendael Museum. The museum displays Native American artifacts, as well as mementos of Delaware's seafaring past. On the third Saturday of June, the town of Milton hosts the Delmarva Hot Air Balloon Festival and Craft Festival. Visitors can even take a ride in a balloon.

We'll end our tour of Delaware near the town of Laurel, where you can see the Great Cypress Swamp in Trap Pond State Park. This swamp contains one of the largest stands of bald cypress trees in the United

States. Although access to the swamp is limited, some roads offer a sneak peek of the swamp's natural beauty.

Despite its small size, Delaware has much to see and do. From biking and hiking, to museums and plays, there's something for everyone in Delaware.

(opposite)
A man in traditional Nanticoke dress gets ready for a powwow.

DELAWARE ALMANAC

Statehood date and number: December 7, 1787/1st

State seal: Features the Delaware coat of arms surrounded by the inscription, "Great Seal of the State of Delaware," and the dates 1793, 1847, and 1907. (The dates mark major changes to the state seal.) Adopted in 1777.

State flag: A background of colonial blue surrounding a diamond in which the coat of arms is placed. Below the diamond are the words, "December 7, 1787," the day on which Delaware was the first state to ratify the United States Constitution. Adopted in 1913.

Geographic center: Kent County, 11 miles (18 km) south of Dover

Total area/rank: 2,489 square miles (6,446 sq km)/49th

Coastline: 28 miles (45 km)

Borders: Pennsylvania, Maryland, New Jersey, and the Atlantic Ocean

Latitude and longitude: Delaware is located approximately between 38° 27' to 39° 50' N and 75° 2' to 75° 47' W

Highest/lowest elevation: Ebright Rd., New Castle County, 447.85 ft. (136.5 m) above sea level/sea level along the Atlantic coast

Hottest/coldest temperature: 110°F (38°C) at Millsboro on July 21, 1930/–17°F (–27°C) at Millsboro on January 17, 1893

Land area/rank: 1,982 square miles (5,133 sq km)/49th

Inland water area/rank: 535 square miles (1,386 sq km)/40th

Population/rank (2000 Census): 783,600/45th

Population of major cities:

Wilmington: 72,664

Dover: 32,135

Newark: 28,547

Origin of state name: Named after Lord De La Warr, Governor of Virginia

State capital: Dover

Previous capitals: New Castle (1704–1777)

Counties: New Castle, Kent, Sussex

State government: 21 senators, 41 representatives

Major rivers/lakes: Delaware River, Christina River, Brandywine Creek, Smyrna River, Nanticoke River, Pocomoke River/Lums Pond, Trap Pond

Farm products: Soybeans, potatoes, corn, mushrooms, lima beans, green peas, barley, cucumbers, and wheat

Livestock: Broiler chickens, hogs, sheep, and cattle

Manufactured products: Chemicals, nylon, clothing, luggage, paper, rubber, plastic, autos, processed meats and vegetables, railroad and aircraft equipment

Mining products: Crushed stone, sand, gravel, and magnesium

Fishing products: Weakfish, crabs, clams, sea bass, and carp

Beverage: Milk

Bird: Blue hen chicken

Bug: Ladybug

Colors: Colonial blue and buff

Fish: Sea trout (weakfish)

Flower: Peach blossom

Mineral: Sillimanite

Motto: Liberty and Independence

Nickname: The First State, also known as the Diamond State, the Blue Hen State, Small Wonder

Song: "Our Delaware," written by George B. Hynson, music by William M. S. Brown

Tree: American holly

Wildlife: Deer, foxes, beavers, rabbits, muskrats, otters, turtles, horseshoe crabs, weakfish, clams, crabs, sturgeon, bass, eels, carp, pickerel, woodpeckers, orioles, snow geese, eagles, hawks, duck, cardinals, and many other kinds of mammals, fish, and birds

TIMELINE

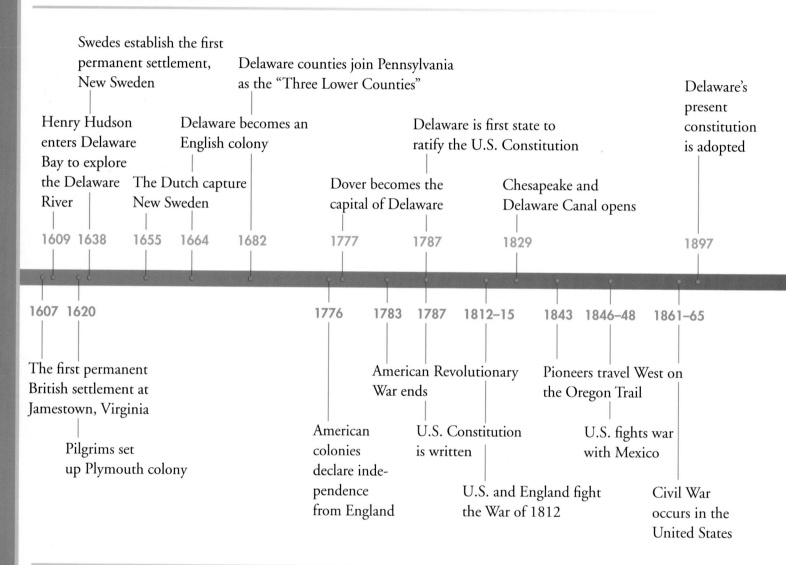

Swedes establish the first permanent settlement, New Sweden

Delaware counties join Pennsylvania as the "Three Lower Counties"

Delaware's present constitution is adopted

Henry Hudson enters Delaware Bay to explore the Delaware River

Delaware becomes an English colony

Delaware is first state to ratify the U.S. Constitution

The Dutch capture New Sweden

Dover becomes the capital of Delaware

Chesapeake and Delaware Canal opens

1609   1638   1655   1664   1682   1777   1787   1829   1897

1607 1620   1776   1783   1787   1812–15   1843   1846–48   1861–65

The first permanent British settlement at Jamestown, Virginia

American Revolutionary War ends

Pioneers travel West on the Oregon Trail

Pilgrims set up Plymouth colony

American colonies declare independence from England

U.S. Constitution is written

U.S. fights war with Mexico

U.S. and England fight the War of 1812

Civil War occurs in the United States

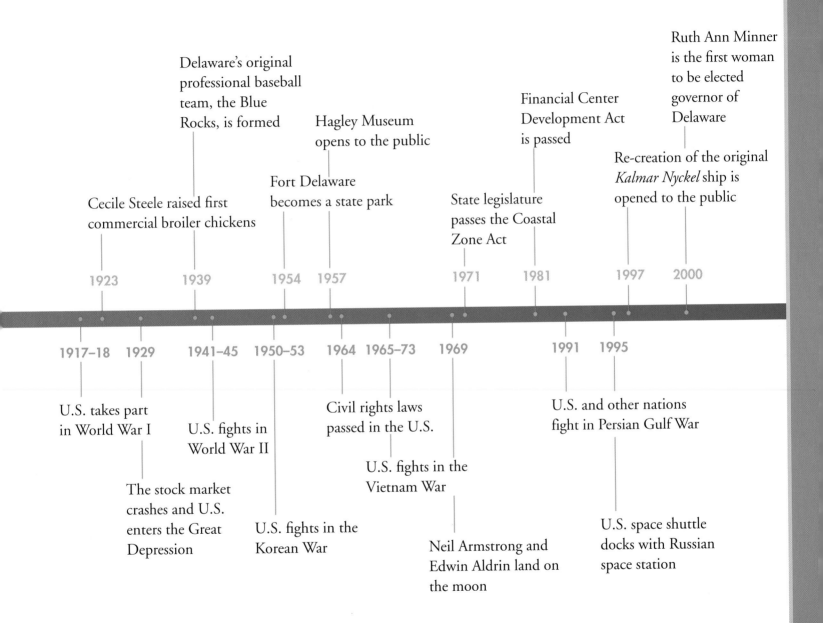

Delaware's original
professional baseball
team, the Blue
Rocks, is formed

Hagley Museum
opens to the public

Financial Center
Development Act
is passed

Ruth Ann Minner
is the first woman
to be elected
governor of
Delaware

Fort Delaware
becomes a state park

State legislature
passes the Coastal
Zone Act

Re-creation of the original
Kalmar Nyckel ship is
opened to the public

Cecile Steele raised first
commercial broiler chickens

1923　　　1939　　　1954　1957　　　1971　　　1981　　　1997　2000

1917–18　1929　　1941–45　1950–53　1964　1965–73　1969　　　1991　1995

U.S. takes part
in World War I

The stock market
crashes and U.S.
enters the Great
Depression

U.S. fights in
World War II

U.S. fights in the
Korean War

Civil rights laws
passed in the U.S.

U.S. fights in the
Vietnam War

Neil Armstrong and
Edwin Aldrin land on
the moon

U.S. and other nations
fight in Persian Gulf War

U.S. space shuttle
docks with Russian
space station

GALLERY OF FAMOUS DELAWAREANS

Thomas F. Bayard
(1828–1898)
United States senator who represented Delaware from 1869 to 1885, and United States secretary of state from 1885 to 1889. Born in Wilmington.

Henry S. Canby
(1878–1961)
Editor, writer, and teacher at Yale University. He helped found a top literary magazine called the *Literary Review*. Born in Wilmington.

Mary Ann Shadd Cary
(1823–1893)
Founded schools for African-American children in Delaware and Pennsylvania. She was the first female African-American newspaper editor (for *Provincial Freeman*) in North America. Born in Wilmington.

Felix Darley
(1821–1888)
World-famous illustrator and painter. Lived in Claymont.

Alfred I. du Pont
(1864–1935)
Businessman who helped to rescue his family's failing company in 1902. Born near Wilmington.

Henry Algernon du Pont
(1838–1926)
United States senator who represented Delaware from 1906 to 1917. Born near Wilmington.

Henry Francis du Pont
(1880–1969)
He founded the Winterthur Museum in 1951. Born in Winterthur.

Pierre Samuel du Pont
(1870–1954)
Helped transform DuPont into a chemical corporation. He also worked for higher education standards in Delaware. Born in Wilmington.

Henry Heimlich
(1920–)
Physician who developed a procedure to help people who are choking. Born in Wilmington.

Daniel Nathans
(1928–1999)
Physician and biologist who won the Nobel Prize for medicine in 1978. Born in Wilmington.

GLOSSARY

ancient: a time long ago

broiler chicken: a young bird suitable for cooking that weighs up to 2.5 pounds (1.1 kilograms)

canal: a manmade waterway that links two bodies of water

capital: a city that is the seat of government

capitol: the building where the government meets

climate: the weather of a particular region over a long period of time

constitution: a written statement outlining the basic laws by which a country or state is organized

economy: the production and exchange of good and services

explorer: someone who visits and studies new lands

financial: relating to banks and money

fossil: the remains of an animal or plant that lived a long time ago

industry: business activity that employs many workers

integrate: to end racial segregation by giving full, equal membership in a group

legislature: the branch of government that makes laws

peninsula: a narrow piece of land that juts out from the mainland into a sea or lake

plain: a large expanse of flat dry land, usually with few trees

plateau: a high, level piece of land

population: the number of people living in a certain location

ratify: to approve

secede: to withdraw from

segregation: the separation of races

surveyor: a person whose job is to examine land for the purpose of making a map

tourism: the business of providing services for visitors, such as food and lodging

wildlife refuge: a place where animals are protected

FOR MORE INFORMATION

Web sites

First State Online
http://www.delaware.gov/
Information about the government of Delaware.

Grandma's Attic Kid's Museum at the Delaware History Museum
http://www.hsd.org/kidsdiscvr.htm
Links to the Delaware History Museum, facts about Delaware, and other historical information about the state.

Welcome to Delaware
http://www.visitdelaware.net
Official site of the Delaware tourism office.

Books

Fradin, Dennis. *The Delaware Colony* (The Thirteen Colonies). Danbury, CT: Children's Press, 1992.

Melchiore, Susan. *Caesar Rodney: American Patriot* (Colonial Leaders). Broomall, PA: Chelsea House Publishers, 2000.

Stein, R. Conrad. *The Underground Railroad.* Danbury, CT: Children's Press, 1997.

Addresses

Delaware Chamber of Commerce
1200 N. Orange St., Suite 200
Wilmington, DE 19899-0671

Delaware Historical Society
504 Market Street
Wilmington, DE 19801

The Fort Delaware Society
P.O. Box 553
Delaware City, DE 19706

Delaware Tourism Office
99 Kings Highway
Dover, DE 19903

INDEX

ABOUT THE AUTHOR

Amy Miller is a writer and editor living in New York City. She has written articles and plays for children about many subjects and topics. To write this story of the First State, she read as many books and articles as she could find. She also found lots of information on the Internet.